The Painting of Pictures

by Arthur Zaidenberg

THE WORLD PUBLISHING COMPANY

CLEVELAND AND NEW YORK

Published by The World Publishing Company
2231 West 110th Street, Cleveland, Ohio 44102
Published simultaneously in Canada by
Nelson, Foster & Scott Ltd.

Library of Congress Catalog Card Number: 66-24999

FIRST EDITION

Printed in the United States of America.

ACKNOWLEDGMENTS

Grateful acknowledgment is made to the following for permission to reproduce the illustrations in this book:

Beilin Gallery — "Awakening" by Jan De Ruth. Photographed by Ann Racz. Reprinted by permission.

— — — "Chapters End" by Jan De Ruth. Photographed by Ann Racz. Reprinted by permission.

— — — "Quartet" by Jan De Ruth. Photographed by Ann Racz. Reprinted by permission.

— — — "Sea Shells" by Jan De Ruth. Photographed by Ann Racz. Reprinted by permission.

Collection of Mr. and Mrs. William Gotz — "Still Life with Palette" by Sigmund Menkes. Reprinted by permission.

Hammer Galleries — "Dublin Horse Show" by LeRoy Neiman. Reprinted by permission.

— — — "Polo at Windsor" by LeRoy Neiman. Reprinted by permission.

— — — "Spectator Fleet, Newport" by LeRoy Neiman. Reprinted by permission.

Mary Hunt, photographer — "The Hammock" by Tommy Beere. Reprinted by permission.

Peter A. Juley & Sons, photographers — "Gulls" by Tommy Beere. Reprinted by permission.

Collection of Beatrice Leval — "The Senegals" by Tommy Beere. Reprinted by permission.

— — — "Self-Portrait as a Golf Player" by Yasuo Kuniyoshi. Reprinted by permission.

— — — "The Starry Night" by Vincent van Gogh. Reprinted by permission.

— — — "Still Life with Apples" by Paul Cézanne. Reprinted by permission.

— — — "Three Women at the Spring" by Pablo Picasso. Reprinted by permission.

Contents

INTRODUCTION

In many ways the seemingly huge white canvas seems identical to the endless, parched desert that confronts the lost prospector. The artist, too, begins to see mirages; the wraiths of beautiful pictures pass before his eyes and disappear only to be replaced by a series of other images. In the best sense, the blank canvas is already a picture. It is perfectly spaced, balanced, and serene. To violate it with a careless brush stroke seems unthinkable in the first minutes of confrontation. Then, one of the mirages begins to take hold and become clarified in the mind of the painter. A pressing need to fix that image on canvas possesses him and he cannot be restrained in his intent to trap that image. The process described is a healthy one. The artist should respect that clean space as virgin territory not to be treated lightly. If he feels his responsibility keenly his respect will inevitably appear in his picture.

Too often we see paintings smashed thoughtlessly and egotistically upon the canvas. Nature's plant fibers, combined with the weaver's skill and the primer's surfacing patina, are covered forever with crude daubs applied by uninspired brushes. If a single fault can be named that would contribute most flagrantly to a bad picture, it would be emotional apathy on the part of the painter.

This book will place few restrictions upon the student, but this is one that must be stated and insisted upon: Never paint when you are bored. It will show in every stroke.

A synonym for the bored painter is the *uninspired* painter, but the word must be clearly defined. Inspiration does not necessarily mean a spiritual message from the ether, nor a gift of genius endowed at birth. Anyone who can love and hate, laugh and cry, or experience *any* deep emotional response possesses the first ingredient for inspiration. To this basic component, add the ability to think honestly and clearly, to imagine and envision, and you have the substances from which inspirations are formed.

The qualities listed may be possessed in varying degrees. All of us are not equally endowed. But, for most working purposes, you have them if you are interested in painting pictures and you must have them if you are now turning the pages of this book.

This book is not intended simply as another "how-to-paint" book. As the title implies, the word "picture" has a special connotation. The painting of a picture calls for a respectful approach and a deep feeling of responsibility to oneself and to those who will be confronted with that picture. All too often the vanity of the artist (a necessary ingredient, and a virtue, if combined with self-critical honesty) causes him to send out into the bewildered world some ill-considered effusion, some carelessly tossed-off sketch he calls a picture. His ego conveniently allows him to accept anything he scribbles as automatically worthy and the world must therefore accept it unquestioningly. With a curious inverse modesty he reasons, "Who is to question what God hath wrought?" Whatever his inspired hand has touched belongs to the ages.

Fortunately, the serious artist is more discriminating. His making of a picture requires inner searching and outer planning. I have known artists to repaint, scrape out, and do a dozen versions of a concept before they felt that the "picture status" had been reached. A picture should be the culmination—Cézanne called it the "realization"—of the combined elements of sketches and studies, compositional planning (and replanning) and, most important, the highest intensity of emotion and inspiration the artist can summon to his aid.

Then should follow a period of withholding from the public until the artist feels his newborn child is worthy of bearing his name. Only then may he call his work a picture and send it out into the world. His relatives, the public, and the critics may then like it or not. But he has satisfied himself. He has given his honest all.

This book will deal with elements of picture making learned through the long experience of seeing and loving good pictures. Add to that a life of devotion to the painting process and serious efforts to paint honestly. Learning can be imparted to a certain extent and these pages will try to do that.

In the final analysis, the best teacher will be the student's own experience, but it is hoped that careful use of these pages will give the student sound equipment to guide him over the rough path toward picture painting.

I would, at this point, like to approach a subject that might at first seem out of place in an instructional book such as this one. The subject is fear.

Fear is the great enemy of the beginner. Many potentially fine painters have been lost to us through the terrors confronting them at the outset of their painting adventures. The tired line, "I can't draw a straight line," is heard ad nauseam from otherwise intelligent adults. The ability to draw a straight line has never been part of the equipment of any artist, but this is often the first fearful expression from those who have never tried to express themselves in paint. Others, all too frequently, are driven to abandon their promising start into the creative world through diffidence engendered by the fantastic skills and monumental accomplishments of the masters. The masters deserve deep respect, but don't let yourself suffer by making tormenting comparisons. When the rare talents of the great prevent the self-expression of the beginner, they are serving purposes they themselves never intended.

To draw a comparison, it would be a sorry state of affairs if couples gave up having children because of the unlikelihood of those children becoming Aristotles or Einsteins. Your pictures can be vital without attaining lofty stature. Few of us complain that the ancient Greeks produced a disproportionately large number of fine artists. Nor do we disparage the Renaissance for its thousands of masters, major and minor.

Bear in mind that in Greece, the small city-state of Athens produced artists by the hundreds. Some mysterious combination of uninhibiting ingredients liberated vast sources of creative energy. If such uninhibiting action would occur in every age we would be far richer. The expression "Fools rush in where angels fear to tread" must not haunt us with its stultifying implications. Let us have more fearless "fools" and rely less upon "angels." Love, admire, and learn from the masters, but be *your own* master. At least to the point where you have given your potential for self-expression the fullest try.

Another inhibiting agent is the imagined complexity of the artist's materials, the vast range of paraphernalia produced for artists by art suppliers. The fact is that the tools of the artist are proliferating to the point of suffocating many beginners and bewildering many more. The humble, faithful oil paints, universally obtainable, are still the basic painting materials, as are simple water colors. Experimentation with the plastics and acrylics, encaustics, polymers, and the countless other media may be enticing, but put off your experimenting until familiarity with basic media makes the painting process less terrifying.

We shall concentrate mostly on painting pictures with oils. Do not become overwhelmed by feats performed by great oil technicians. Familiarize yourself with the feel of brushes, palette knife, or whatever applicator you are most comfortable with. Then forget materials. It is the picture that counts.

THE PAINTING OF PICTURES

WHY PAINT PICTURES?

Believe it or not, the question "Why paint pictures?" arises even among painters of long years of dedication. Despite the relatively recent (and growing) public interest in art, the painter encounters amazing indifference to many of his effusions by relatives, friends, and ninety-nine per cent of the world's population. Not only does he suffer this, but, even worse, he must also answer (daily) the perturbing questions that arise in his mind regarding the validity of his own works. If he copes successfully with these ego-deflating conditions he must then face the fact that, with few exceptions, the monetary returns from painting are likely to be meager in comparison, say, to those of a job on Wall Street or even those of a college professor. Fortunately these practical considerations have rarely prevented "paint-touched" characters from flinging themselves into the precarious profession of the artist.

Many books have been written on painting. I have contributed quite a few books on that theme. In them, and in any such book worthy of notice, certain qualifications are stressed:

1. A love of art and the artist's point of view must be present in the prospective painter.
2. A deep respect for the complex media of the artist and a willingness to learn to handle them.
3. An honest desire to say something in paint.
4. An honest effort to see with the eye of the artist.

With these prerequisites any intelligent person can learn to paint pictures of basic merit, and in some cases excellent and even great pictures.

Each of us sees things in his own special fashion. Our viewpoints are filtered through our experiences, opinions, the intensity of our enthusiasm, and a vast range of other impacts on our vision. The artist must acquire a special vision that channels almost every one of those impacts toward pictorial expression. In his lifetime an artist may paint only a few hundred pictures but he "sees" thousands.

This condition is one of the rewards of the art student and it reaches even greater heights in the life of the full-time artist. The greatest reward and the true answer to the question "Why paint pictures?" is the intense satisfaction of expression on canvas of one's special viewpoint and emotion. Those rare occasions when one succeeds in this accomplishment provide rewards equal, in a sense, to striking oil or falling in love. When, in addition, one wins the applause and recognition of a discerning element of the public, one's cup is full indeed.

A picture need not be complex because it is the result of a culmination of study, plans, and inspired emotional painting. A painting of an apple, properly placed on the canvas against a flat, one-color background may convey as much emotion as a painting of a teeming street crowd. Emotion is not to be depicted literally. The painted tears on a cheap oleograph of a Madonna are less evocative of emotion than a sunflower by Van Gogh or an apple by Cézanne. The exact nature of the process of evoking emotional responses is not traceable, but it is certainly true that emotional painting produces emotional responses in the viewer. Excitement engenders excitement, no matter what the theme.

Although this book is not intended as an instruction book in techniques, methods of color mixing, and other how-to-paint steps, but rather one that will help direct the student toward the conceiving of pictures, a review of some of the elements that add directly to that purpose would not be amiss.

Paint application, at least such elements as apply to the textural contribution to the picture surface, is a vital study. The use of form and figure structure, where it applies to the construction of the picture composition, is important. Color, in terms of picture making, is relevant as it relates with other colors to make a whole that enhances the picture. These elements should be studied as they appear in the plates throughout the book.

YOUR WORKSHOP
AND TOOLS

No serious artist has ever abandoned his work because he lacked a comfortable, north-lighted studio.

Many of the greatest creative works were painted in shabby, cold attics or cellars. This is not to imply that such conditions are a prerequisite to the creation of paintings. It is meant to stress the fact that anyone who loves to paint will do so under any conditions, in any space available. However, it is well to set up as adequate a work area as you can. Material and space arrangements should be as functional as possible. The problems that beset the artist are sufficiently pressing without the addition of avoidable chaos.

A sturdy easel is desirable. A spacious slab of smooth wood or glass makes a suitable palette. For the lazy artist there have been developed the wax-paper pad and palette. After each painting session the page may be ripped off and discarded.

The painting table next to the easel should be large enough to hold in readiness tubes of paint, palette, brush, jars, and other materials.

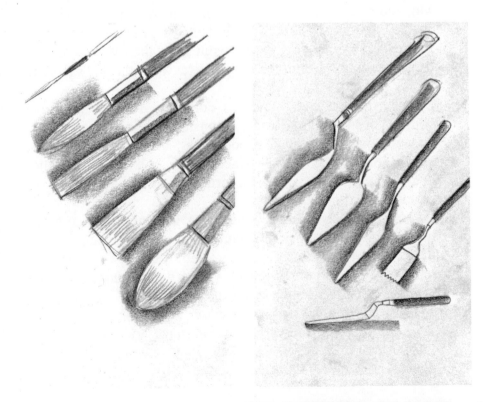

The chart opposite depicts the basic tools for the studio.

1. Three easels are shown:
   A. A folding easel for sketching trips in preparation for studio work.
   B. An inexpensive studio easel, which is quite adequate.
   C. A good studio easel is more expensive, but is a good investment if you plan large paintings.
2. Canvas. If you can afford linen canvas it is preferable to cotton. Linen is more durable and resilient. However, for most paint sketching inexpensive cotton is adequate. Canvas-covered cardboard panels are even less expensive than stretched cotton canvases. They are good for sketching, are sturdy, and are space-savers.
3. Charcoal sticks. These are used for drawing on the canvas before painting.
4. Oil and turpentine cups. These should clip onto the palette securely.
5. Good-sized bottles of linseed oil and turpentine. You will certainly use considerable quantities if you do as much painting as you should.
6. A dozen brushes of various size and character suitable for your special needs. They should range from small pointed-tip brushes to broad, flat, or rounded ones. You will soon find your favorites.
7. Palette knife. Some artists prefer to apply paint to their canvases with the pliant palette knife rather than with brushes. Others combine the two. The knife may be used to mix colors on the palette and for scraping excess paint from the canvas. Another use is for scraping paint from the palette when the day's painting is over.
8. Palette. It may be a luxurious curved and polished, "store-bought" beauty that will make you feel like a real artist or it may be a smooth slab of wood, glass, or porcelain. Any relatively nonabsorbent hard surface will do, as long as it will allow you to range your paints comfortably and give you plenty of space for mixing.
9. Have plenty of clean rags available. Oil painting (or any kind of painting) is a messy procedure and requires much cleaning during and afterward. Otherwise your studio will get out of hand. Brushes require frequent wiping during painting. Heavy residues of pigment must be removed frequently.
10. A paint box for your tubes of color. As your painting career develops you will widen your color range and tubes will pile up in quantities. Get a box large enough to hold your tubes along with brushes, knives, and other tools.

 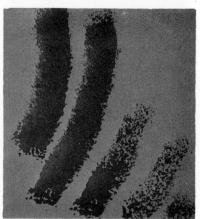

6   THE PAINTING OF PICTURES

OIL PAINTING

The popularity of painting in oil colors over all other media has its reasons. There is a sensuous charm and a plastic quality to the material that gives pleasure to the user aside from its quality as a medium for expression. The physical pleasure involved in handling oils lies partly in the fact that not only is it a coloring material but it also has a sculptural character. Working with understanding and sympathy the painter in oils can build and model on his canvas, in addition to creating a wide range of beautiful variations of tone and color. Oils became the chief medium of painters as long ago as the fifteenth century and have remained the dominant material for artists of the western hemisphere.

No other medium is quite as versatile and tractable. The tones of oil paints do not change materially from the moment of wet application to the point of complete drying, years later. When dry, the paint looks as fresh as on the day of its mixing. The drying process is very slow and the artist is never pressed to "finish" passages because of the imminent changes in the nature of the paint as he applies stroke after stroke. He may make changes and mixtures on the canvas thoughtfully and he is not driven to use flashy speed approaches to adjust to the intractable qualities so prevalent in tempera and water-solvent paints. The artist may build up in layers or he may paint in spontaneous single-coat brilliance, but the choice is his and does not depend on the exigencies of the medium.

Another of the many virtues of oil, possibly its greatest, is that there is no *one* method of using it. There are as many techniques of oil painting as there are painters in oil. It may be applied smoothly or flung on to the canvas with the thickness of plaster. Colors may be flowed on with luminous transparency or used with deep opacity. Glazes, or transparent layer upon layer, can be used to produce subtle blendings—or the color may be applied in stipples or gobs, sculpturesque in their impasto or structural in their modeling.

The range of color possible in oil pigments seems unlimited, allowing each painter to be an individual. Any two artists would find it very difficult to handle oil paints in exactly the same fashion. Forging the application and mixing of paint calls for long study and can only be performed by expert forgers.

THE APPLICATION OF PAINT

Just as with handwriting, the "brush writing" of no two artists is exactly the same. Experts in detecting fraudulent paintings are able to make comparisons of the brush strokes of the real painting and the forgery and reach absolute conclusions. Unfortunate as it is for the forger, it is one of the many factors that make for the rich variety of paintings in the world.

Many an art student, deeply impressed by a teacher will, consciously or unconsciously, try to paint in the same manner. In his efforts to do so he will often succeed in emulating the actual application of paint to a certain extent. Fortunately, these acquired mannerisms usually wear off as the student's own personality takes over and self-confidence is asserted. Such early influences are not necessarily bad. They are often instructive if honest admiration is the motivating force rather than the desire to cash in on the fame of another or to pass off spurious copies of another artist's works. It would be hard to find a painter, even among the masters, who has not been influenced to a degree by some other painter.

One of the unfortunate aspects of the contemporary art scene is the lack of individuality on the part of students who in their anxiety to enter into the professional exhibiting arena skip the period of self-discovery and drip, throw, or scribble paint in emulation of others who have arrived at their special approach through their own honest search for a special form of expression.

Look at good pictures, enjoy them, admire them, study their qualities and techniques. There is a great deal to learn from them, but be yourself. Your "brush writing" is not only a peculiarity of your own, it is the distillation of all your thoughts and emotions. Do not squander that heritage in an attempted exchange for someone else's personality in paint.

10   THE PAINTING OF PICTURES

IMPASTO

Impasto is an important word frequently used in describing the surface of paintings. It refers to the thickness and the character of the pigment applied to the canvas by brush, palette knife, paint roller, or thrown, dripped, or otherwise transferred to canvas. The character of the impasto is a very important contribution to the picture. The nature of the impasto is an intrinsic part of the brush-handwriting of the artist. Some of its personal qualities are unconsciously applied and are traceable in every work of every consistent artist.

But the choice of the nature of the impasto most suitable to the subject and emotions of each painting is each artist's privilege and is a very important decision. In a way, the impasto is an addition of an actual dimension to the painting. It gives, in a subtle way, a sculptural quality to the painting's surface. Varied in thickness and character on the canvas, it can contribute strongly to the design and movement of the composition. More important still, it is a vital contribution to the emotional impact of the picture. It is obvious that the impasto with which the serene beauty of a Vermeer interior was painted would be unsuited to the passion and anger of a painting by Chaim Soutine. The pale, delicate depravity suggested in a Pascin's paint cannot be applied in expressing the violent reactions of Van Gogh.

As stated, all the artist's tools for applying paint contribute to the impasto, but certain tools are more suited to the application of heavy impasto. A tiny, pointed brush obviously cannot be used for strong, heavily applied paint. A palette knife is ineffective for delicate, blended surfaces. Wide brushes cannot give the same quality as knife-applied paint. Modern artists have shot paint at the canvas, poured it directly from cans, mixed paints with sand or pebbles, and have even used chemicals mixed with oils that are mutually opposed and that cause a curdling, erupting process to take place. Others use paint rollers—the commercially produced variety used for house painting. Still others use paint sprayers, the common spray-can type or electric-powered sprayers.

I have found that paint rollers of various sizes allow a wide range of paint application in a rich range of thickness. A hard rubber printer's roller about an inch wide is excellent for reasonably delicate work and sponge-rubber rollers as well as textured fabric rollers are excellent for freer paint application.

THE PALETTE KNIFE

For hundreds of years the classic applicator of paint to canvas has been the brush. Growing appreciation for exquisite detail and smooth impasto made the soft, fine-haired brush an indispensable instrument. The process of applying flows of very liquid glazes of color, one over the other, also required the absorbent character of the sable or camel-hair brush.

The masters of the past, with a few robust exceptions such as Frans Hals and El Greco, could not have used so free-swinging a tool as the palette knife in applying paint to their greatly detailed work. During the last hundred years or so several schools of painting developed whose approach did not require delicate surfaces and great detail painting. The impressionists, postimpressionists, cubists, and their many offspring schools allowed painters considerably more freedom in paint application and the fine brush ceased to be the only painting instrument.

With the palette knife rich daubs of pigment may be applied and spread on the canvas. Obviously the knife cannot hold very liquid, flowing pigment—paint thus applied would be opaque. The resultant impasto is relatively heavy and the palette knife may be used much in the same manner as the tools used in modeling clay.

The palette knife is made in many sizes and with variations of pliancy of its steel tip. These variations give a considerable range to the character of the impasto applied.

14   THE PAINTING OF PICTURES

PAINTING WITH ROLLERS

Modern artists work in terms that are particularly suited to the use of paint rollers. Typical of contemporary painting is the bold, undetailed application of broad masses of color. This approach does not apply only to painting huge abstract designs. Figurative painters also paint their pictures in relatively simplified terms. Such broad, free qualities are inherent in the nature of paint-roller strokes. Another characteristic of modern painting of several schools is the use of flat areas of color with no effort to "violate" (as they call it) the two-dimensional nature of the canvas surface. Such painting makes no use of perspective, foreground, middle distance, or background to suggest a third dimension, or penetration "into" the canvas.

Again rollers, with their ability to produce flat, even areas of paint, unimpaired by irregular brush strokes and streaks left by the hairs of the brush produce the desired flatness with ease.

Still another character, typical of modern painting, is the large size of many works, both abstract and figure paintings. Here again, the use of paint rollers allows the solid coverage of large areas with directness, precision, and speed, which is of considerable importance. Speed is important because artists are very often bored by the chore of filling in large areas of color with the usual, relatively narrow brush strokes and the small paint load carried on a brush. This list of the broad, free qualities of the roller's strokes does not imply that they cannot be used, with some practice, for detailed and even minute areas and for sharp-edged and "line" painting. In short, I have found that paint rollers have all the versatility required for most painting problems.

You will find, in this book, much comment on impasto. Considering that this is not a book on how to paint, it should be explained that although color mixing and blending, figure construction, etc., are not our province, impasto differences deal with the very nature of the picture in somewhat the same way as modeling differs from stone sculpture. For that reason the technique of paint-roller application of impasto follows in some detail.

Paint-roller handles are permanent. The roller covers are sturdy, but when they become worn they may be removed from the roller and replaced inexpensively.

The preliminary covering of the canvas is accomplished with greater speed by using a roller and the covering quality is also more uniform and less inclined to leave lumps and ridges of paint than the brush. Also, the texture, "tooth," and thickness of the covering are more controllable with the roller.

The results obtained with rollers are "different" from those obtained with brushwork. Difference in itself is of small importance unless that difference contains virtues of its own—then the difference becomes valid. Painting pictures with rollers produces effects, blendings of color, varieties of paint texture, and "sculptural" qualities of modeling quite unlike those produced by brushwork. The reasons for the special character and different nature of the results from those of brushwork painting lie in the essential difference of the two varieties of painting tools.

Brushes are made of hundreds of hairs or bristles bound together. Roller covers are made of many varieties of material very dissimilar to those used for brushes. Roller covers suitable for artists are made of lambs wool or Dacron fibers, foam rubber, carpeting material, and mohair, as well as several synthetic plastic products. The choice is wide and each kind of cover produces a texture on the canvas unobtainable with brushes.

Your work table will require some changes from the conventional brush-painting arrangements. The palette should be larger than the normal painting palette in order to give space in which to manipulate the roller freely in the paint-saturating or mixing process. A slab of glass, porcelain, or metal about 2 feet by 2½ feet makes a good palette.

Collect several old coffee cans—the low, broad types make good containers for liquid thinner and for containing water or solvents for cleaning roller covers. The cans should be ranged close to your palette. The broad, flat synthetic sponges used in kitchens are helpful in rolling excess liquid from rollers. A stack of old newspapers serves a similar purpose. Use both a sponge and newspaper. A rack should be used against which to lean your rollers during painting.

Now for the actual painting tools. Your equipment should include four rollers of varying size and texture.

These should be sufficient for most painting projects. They are planned to deal with broad areas of painting as well as with most details. If you are inclined to use some tiny detail or especially fine lines in painting you will require a fine, pointed brush.

When you have chosen among the various commercially produced pigments, whether oil or water colors, you will need a palette knife for scooping gobs of paint from jars or for mixing colors on the palette. The palette knife also serves as a scraper for removing leftover pigments from the palette when cleaning up.

Charcoal sticks are commonly used by artists for underdrawing on canvas because the marks easily brush off when no longer required as guide lines, and, when painting over has begun, they are harmlessly absorbed by the pigment.

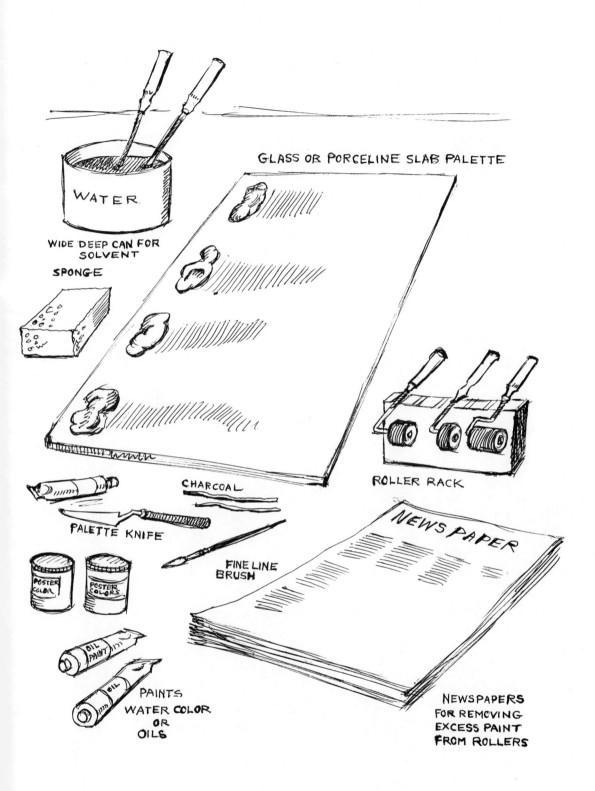

WATER

WIDE DEEP CAN FOR
SOLVENT

SPONGE

GLASS OR PORCELINE SLAB PALETTE

ROLLER RACK

CHARCOAL

PALETTE KNIFE

FINE LINE
BRUSH

POSTER COLOR

POSTER COLORS

OIL PAINT

OIL

PAINTS
WATER COLOR
OR
OILS

NEWS PAPER

NEWSPAPERS
FOR REMOVING
EXCESS PAINT
FROM ROLLERS

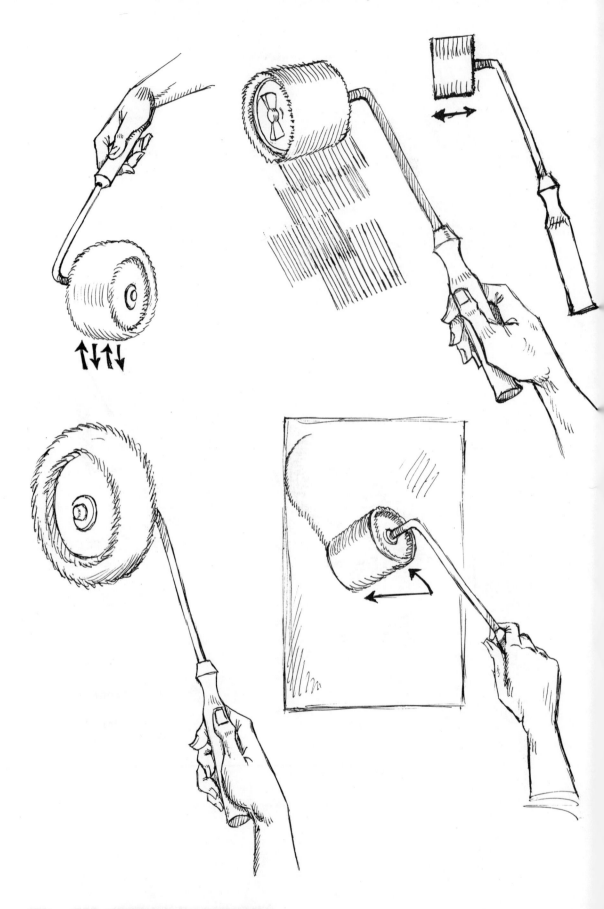

Range your paint gobs on the palette slab, well separated, along the far edge of the palette. Mixing one color with another may be done with your palette knife, again allowing a generous space between the newly mixed color and the other gobs of color. Pick up a dab of the required color with your roller and then, using no more pressure than the weight of the roller, roll the paint into the roller cover by back-and-forth passes on the palette just below the source of the color dab, until the roller is evenly saturated, not too thickly and not too dripping wet as to be uncontrollable.

Now apply the saturated roller to the canvas with light-pressured, springy strokes. This will produce textured areas of color on the canvas. Proceed to paint very much in the same manner as with brushes. Some mixing may be accomplished directly on the canvas with the roller. In other cases you may want to use a clean roller for each color to be applied.

You will find it easier in the early stages of painting with rollers to choose subjects that require a minimum of small detail. The strong, broad strokes applied with the roller aid many artists in their efforts to escape from the fussy, over-detailed painting often induced by the pointed, narrow nature of brushes. Painting is not merely a continuance of the drawing process, which is essentially done with sharp-pointed pencils, charcoal, or pens. Modern painting, particularly, has allowed for strong, bold application of paint and a vital painting quality of that nature is implicit in the paint-rolling procedure.

This does not mean that, after some practice, the small paint roller cannot be used for detailed features in the painting. Narrow strokes and small dabs of paint may be achieved by "leaning" the roller, with a slight lift toward one end or the other of the roller—the finer the stroke required, the higher the "tilt."

Do not be discouraged if you are not adroit in controlling the roller immediately. Remember your awkward brushwork when you first used the long-handled artist's brushes.

The practice required in acquiring dexterity with the roller will be very rewarding and not too time-consuming. You will soon find that you are accomplishing form by building strokes and achieving textural structure more easily than you could with the brush.

For the most part you will find yourself using the full width of the roller, well saturated with paint, when rolling the color on in broad strokes. These strokes may be used almost as building blocks are used in construction. Most forms may be "built," almost sculpturally, utilizing broad squares and oblongs of solid paint. Do not put too much pressure on the roller in this "building" process since it will wear down the nap of the roller fabric.

Through practice you will soon find the various texture-producing quality of each fabric on your roller covers.

You will find that the best of these features will be brought out by applying very little pressure to the handle of the roller when painting. Make full use of the thick pile of the "furry" fabrics and the pattern in the weaves of the carpet material fabric. Foam-rubber rollers are excellent for smooth areas of painting.

Broad strokes are achieved with the full surface of the roller; narrow paint lines are accomplished by tilting at an angle so as to use the sharp edge of the roller. The less the angle of the tilt, the broader the paint stroke. Lines or narrow strokes are best produced by foam-rubber rollers.

Use your roller not only in its obvious roll-on fashion but also as a "tamping" tool. Paint applied in this fashion produces soft, textured impasto with a "tooth" that results from dab-and-pull-away tamping. The light metal shaft of the roller handle and the springy nature of the cover fabrics permit the painter to produce fresh, spontaneous impasto on the canvas. Utilize this "bounce" quality of the roller and notice that the pigment does not have the overworked, scrubbed-on look so often produced by the brush.

In this simple composition the paint has been rolled on with broad, free strokes and the painting was "finished" in a few moments. While speed is not a great virtue in painting, the ability to accomplish the statement in paint that the artist wishes to make, with a minimum of fussy brush strokes (so often destructive to the strength and spontaneity of that statement) is highly desirable.

SEE COLORPLATE ON PAGE **132**

This cat sketch was done with a combination of virtually all the strokes readily available to the artist using rollers.

The tilted roller was used to accomplish lines and narrow strokes. This paint was rolled on, stroked on, tamped on, and "roller brushed on" (roller brushing may be accomplished with short sweeps of the tilted roller sidewise instead of using the wheeling turn of the roller).

SEE COLORPLATE ON PAGE **133**

This head is an example of the blending of colors possible to the artist with the paint roller. Color lightly rolled over fresh color may be blended directly on the canvas and joined into one soft texture.

24 THE PAINTING OF PICTURES

Luminosity is often attained by allowing the white of the canvas to gleam through thin layers of paint.

The textured roller covers accomplish this with single, spontaneous strokes of the roller on the canvas.

In this head, unlike the head painted with blending colors, paint has been applied with very little rolling of the rollers but rather by "tamping" color from the roller onto the canvas.

The process for removing the paint from your rollers depends on the nature of the pigments used. That difference is dealt with by using the appropriate solvent solution or paint thinner. Rollers used with water colors may be dropped into a can of water and left immersed overnight or rinsed until almost dry and stood on end to dry.

For oil paints, rollers should be immersed in turpentine to commercial paint-removing liquids, but it is not advisable to leave them in such strong solvents over long periods.

For the acrylic polymer paints there are special solvents to be used for stubborn dried paint when water is insufficient. During the painting process, keep a stack of newspapers handy on which to roll off excess paint. Also keep clean rags handy for wiping the rollers almost dry.

I have found that a number of my rollers, through heavy usage, have become saturated with dry paint to the point where they are hard and smooth. These I still use with considerable pleasure and success. A hard, smooth roller surface is effective for some purposes. However, when the naps and textures of the covers wear down or become paint-steeped to the point where they no longer serve your special needs, they are inexpensive enough to be easily replaced. Get a new batch of roller covers.

COMPOSITION

There are no absolutes of compositional rightness that apply in painting pictures. Many theories of composition have evolved through the centuries, but none of them has been anything more than an aid to the unintuitive. They are soon abandoned by the creative artist and are taught as rigid procedures only by the least imaginative teachers. The "pyramidal theory" of composition, the "golden mean" and "dynamic symmetry" are three of those guides that once were popular. Now, in our present day of freedom of expression and encouragement of eccentricity, they are all but obsolete.

This does not mean that the eye-pleasing elements of balance and counterbalance, rhythm and thoughtful juxtapositioning of masses and forms are not to be considered in composing. It is merely suggested that formulas are not finally binding in modern concepts of art, and that emotion and feeling should not be secondary to rigid planning.

Compositions that fall out of the picture plane, forms that crowd upon each other and smother the "living space" and air from a picture, restless movement with no respite for the eye—all these things are certainly to be considered as violation of sound structure, but in the last analysis, the creative artist must make his own decisions based on his taste and reason and above all the needs of his painting "statement."

Certainly the soundest sources of compositional training are the works of the masters, both contemporary and of the past. Every artist whose work you love contributes to your unconscious feeling for composition. *Consciously* study the structure and movement in their works and notice the thought and knowledge they used in creating them.

Here we shall examine some basic structural dos and don'ts. They are the most obvious admonitions and have their values. Composition, like all elements of a picture, is mostly governed by the choice of subject. Obviously, where any amount of realism is used, the depiction of the objects involved, whether landscape, still life, or figures, call for certain spherical forms or horizontals. Since you are your own master in painting you may shift, distort, enlarge, or eliminate those forms that detract from the quality of your composition—but certain disciplines persist.

In nonobjective painting, of course, the composition is not dependent upon the depiction of literal subject matter, therefore there are no restraints other than one's emotions and tastes. These statements are so highly personal that neither the art critic, nor fellow artists may

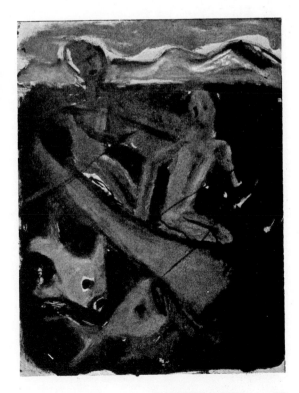

legitimately challenge composition, color, or, for that matter, any part of the content—though that does not prevent them from doing so. There are, however, subconscious as well as intellectual compositional motivations that are employed in the making of good nonobjective paintings, which, while not subject to rules, prevent them from being haphazard daubs, and they evoke responses in the sensitive beholder. It is in the practice of "abstracting" that the true freedom of composition is brought into play. The artist may dissect, dismember, or explode the "real" object and put in elements entirely at the disposal of the sense of composition.

Most abstract artists employ only the two-dimensional surface of the picture area, distaining the "tricks" of perspective, foreshortening, and light and shadow to "penetrate" into the canvas to create the illusion of the third dimension. The relationships of form to form and juxtaposition of color to color to produce the required composition, subordinate all other considerations. Square apples or heads that show both profile and full face at once are permissible if they serve the pictorial needs. Such procedures frequently produce pictures of a power not possible under the restrictions of absolutely realistic portrayal, and such abstracting has not been limited to abstract artists. Many of the old masters took great liberties with the "truths" of nature to enhance the power and intensify the movements in their paintings.

SEE COLORPLATE ON PAGE **134**

THREE-DIMENSIONAL COMPOSITIONS

Compositions that use the simulation of three-dimensional space (as opposed to the flat-picture-plane) use the eye-deceiving devices available to the artist. The major device for suggesting penetration into the distance is that of perspective. Basic perspective, as used by artists, is not a complex procedure requiring long study and intricate drafting tools. Such problems arise for the architectural renderer and draftsman.

We need a simple understanding of the principle of converging lines meeting at a vanishing point on the horizon. We know that railroad tracks seem to narrow as they go off into the distance until they appear to meet at the horizon. This apparent convergence to vanishing points can be applied to all objects where the implication of distance is required. The beholder believes and his eye follows.

The second eye-deceiver is called "foreshortening." This is the principle of convergence used on an object or figure that achieves implication of recession into the distance by exaggerating the portions of the object or figure closest to the beholder's eye and by diminishing those forms that are farther away.

The third method of implying foreground and distance is that of tone of shading. Objects closest to the eye would have the deepest shadows and the brightest highlights. Impression of distance is suggested by the gradual dimming of both the intensity of the light and the depth of the shadows.

The painting below is an example of the implication of three-dimensional space in a street scene. In the line of trees each is somewhat smaller as it recedes into the distance. The diminishing strength of the color, light, and shade in the background, as compared to that of the foreground and the converging lines of the buildings, all contribute to the illusion.

The power or intensity of the local color of objects also contributes to a picture's "penetration." Local color is the intrinsic color of an object, for instance the red of an apple. The local colors dim as they recede into the distance. The following plate gives a demonstration of the principles involved in simple uses of three-dimensional suggestion for compositions.

SEE COLORPLATE ON PAGE **135**

THREE-DIMENSIONAL COMPOSITIONS   33

In this plate, where a vista of receding street lines is not visible, the impression of penetration into the picture plane is achieved by the "movement" of forms that carry the eye back into the distance. The strength or "values" of the color masses also contribute to that impression.

SEE COLORPLATE ON PAGE **136**

In this sketch the figure in the background is considerably smaller, though both are actually the same size in life. This is another device for suggesting penetration in a two-dimensional picture plane to suggest a third dimension, that of distance.

Four paintings by Tommy Beere that demonstrate thoughtful planning of composition combined with fresh, spontaneous painting. . . . . .

Rhythmic use of curves and diagonals.

The Hammock *by Tommy Beere*

The Senegals *by Tommy Beere*

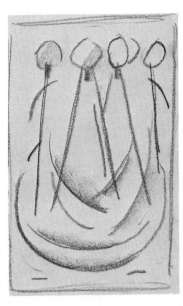

Effective interplay of curves and verticals.

Ring Around a Rosey *by Tommy Beere*

Circular composition in which the movement carries the eye around with the dancers.

Gulls *by Tommy Beere*

Tasteful arrangement of forms.

Self-Portrait as a Golf Player *by Yasuo Kuniyoshi*

Dublin Horse Show *by LeRoy Neiman*

These paintings by LeRoy Neiman cause the eye to "dance" because of the spontaneous vitality of the brush strokes and color.

Spectator Fleet, Newport *by LeRoy Neiman*

Winner at Longchamp *by LeRoy Neiman*

Polo at Windsor *by LeRoy Neiman*

STILL-LIFE PAINTING

The term still life is something of a misnomer. To begin with, flowers and fruit are no less alive than humans or animals. In fact, their intense vitality, so transient, is abundantly evident. The capable artist captures it in his painting. But even a bowl or a chair is vibrant with the air and light about it. These ingredients seen with the emotional eye of the painter can become a very moving thing. Of course, such objects as a shoe or a hat become imbued with the characteristics of the life they have lived and a great deal of the character of their owner. To the alert eye of the painter in search of picture material, nothing is still. Approach your painting of still life with the same searching analysis you would assume before a living model.

The questions to be asked at the outset are: (a) What does the subject say to you? (b) Are you excited by its color, the movement of its directional lines, the human condition in which it resides? (c) This consideration is the most important of all: Would you rather paint it than any other object or subject at the moment? The final question supersedes all others because an artist has innumerable choices he may make for his painting and the choice he does make must be governed only by his deep interest and excitement.

Setting up a still life is a creative act in itself. One must bring into play all one's feeling for composition and color. In part, that is an intuitive procedure, but intuition is only trustworthy to a point.

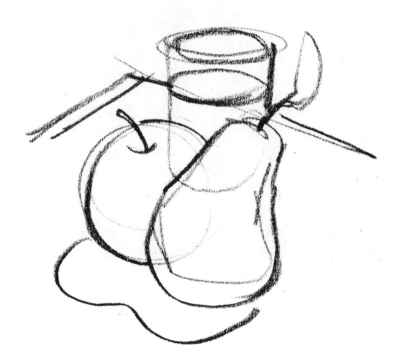

Careful consideration of the factors that contribute to the structure of a good picture are more reliable. Similar problems to those presented by posing a model arise. Are the special qualities of the parts of the still-life group shown to best advantage? Is the "personality" of the orange enhanced by the juxtaposition of the grapes? Is the entire "pose" of the still life true? Is the light cast upon it productive of rich contrasts or subtle interplay?

When you have set up your still life to your satisfaction remember that its "pose" is almost as transient as that of a living person. True, it will not move or fidget as a living model will, but light changes every few minutes and changes the color and in a subtle way even the structure of objects. Make sketches of your still life from various angles, testing its appeal from each viewpoint. Make readjustments in the group if you feel the necessity. When you are satisfied, and if your enthusiasm has not flagged, begin to paint.

There is no formula for how far in detail one should carry a painting. Countless excellent paintings have died when the painter decided to go on after he had said all he need say. If any reliable measure can be applied, it is that a painting is "finished" at the point where inspired emotional painting ceases and mechanical skill takes over.

Determine the source and intensity of light and shade on the area to be used for your still-life arrangement. This is important because the constancy of that lighting will decide the painting time available to you. Quick-changing light sources produce very fleeting shadows and highlights, too transient for leisurely painting.

Many modern artists disdain cast shadows and highlights as contributions to the structure of form. Some are intrigued by the play of translucent light and ephemeral forms. Still others find satisfaction in contrasting deep shadows and lighted planes on still-life objects. The decision must be yours as to the elements of a still-life arrangement and as to the structure that moves you most.

You must devote time and thought to the choice of your still-life subject. Almost any object is of interest to the artist, whether man-made or natural. Your objective should be the placement of objects in a combination of forms and colors in such a way as to produce a dynamic, colorful whole, one worthy of your enthusiastic efforts to capture it on canvas.

To accomplish that end you might spend hours in search and thought, or you might, in the first few minutes of contemplation, hit upon an exciting arrangement. Often the accidental juxtaposition of unrelated objects may inspire an artist to reach for his brushes. More often it is the deliberate placement of objects in a planned structure in which they harmonize and "live together." There can be no set formula for "right" arrangement. Your own highly personal responses will determine that for you. Play with your objects until that response occurs.

"Playing" with rhythms and tones in an effort to find essentials of this still-life arrangement.

The cubists translated all objects into terms of geometric forms. In essence, it is true that all objects are composed of the forms shown here in three-dimensional simulation. In two-dimensional design they become triangles, squares, oblongs, circles, and variations on these basic geometric designs.

Searching for the main "currents" among the infinite number of
leaves, petals, and stems in a flower still life.

Simplicity of subject matter did not detract from the intensity of the emotion nor the architectural and intellectual qualities of this great still life by Cézanne.

Still Life with Apples *by Paul Cézanne*

An emotional still-life painting by Sigmund Menkes, dynamic in its climbing verticals.

Still Life with Palette *by Sigmund Menkes*

LANDSCAPE PAINTING

Every artist invents a new world, inevitably different from the real world about us. Some with exceptional vision, like Picasso or Mondrian, have created worlds that affect our view of the real world as the moon affects the night and the tides. Working creatively, the artist reveals to us a fresh vista. The quality varies but the scene is new and different, and it originates without conscious effort on the part of the artist.

One would suppose that when an artist paints a landscape this "new-world" factor would be severely limited. After all he is painting the natural flora so familiar to us. Fortunately, the limitation is not as severe as one might suppose. No matter how meticulous the painter is he can only paint a fascimile of the landscape before him. Therein lies our good fortune and the heritage of fresh worlds created by the great landscape painters.

Natural sunsets and sunrises are magnificent and awe-inspiring, but they are quite different from those evoked by Turner. His genius created additional thrilling scenes. We have two great spectacles—the "real" and those of the great Turner. There were never "real" landscapes like those of Van Gogh, Sisley, Corot, or Cézanne either, but consider their contribution to the beauty of our world.

When you paint nature you are both handicapped and specially endowed. You lack the materials with which nature fashioned grass, trees, flowers, mountains, etc., but you have mind, heart, wit, and passion, your special handwriting, and your own, sometimes myopic, vision.

Do not despair if your landscape fails to look like the scene before you. Take the observed qualities that prompted you to try to paint that scene, transpose, paraphrase, and intensify them, but above all, select and eliminate. An artist of taste is one up on nature. Nature is anarchic in its vast proliferation, but the concept of beauty is man-made. Nature goes about its procreative business without regard for "picture making." It is only man, the artist, who limits, rearranges, and "stages" the props furnished by nature.

Do not choose a vista for your painting at random. Everything is grist to the artist's mill, but in widely varying degrees. Each landscape painter of note found his special area of interest in nature and that special interest permeates his works. When you have decided upon an area of special interest to you, then you must again employ selectivity.

An aid in selecting an area suitable for transference to canvas is the time-honored two-handed "isolator" shown on the following page.

Some artists cut a square of cardboard similar in shape to the canvas to be used. They peer through it to find the picture area to be painted. Having chosen the limited area of landscape to be painted, the process of elimination must go on. Unlike the poem, in which words are chosen with utmost economy, nature glories in the superfluous. Even the smallest of flowers is a profusion of detail. But the purpose of the painter is not slavish reproduction of nature on canvas. Each square foot of any natural landscape contains innumerable blades of grass, grains of sand, drops of dew, and a myriad of other things. Obviously, a system of artistic shorthand must be used to convey that square foot of landscape. Certainly such a system must be used for the whole complex of natural objects in your complete landscape. It is that shorthand which will contribute mightily to the quality of your painting.

Every vista, whether a broad landscape or a still life set up in your studio, may be reduced to three areas of division, each of which calls for special application of certain basic principles. The foreground is that area which lies closest to the viewer's eye. All objects that lie in this area are relatively larger, though not necessarily *actually* larger, than those which lie in the middle distance. The darks will be darker and the highlights brighter than those in the middle distance. Objects that lie in the middle distance will appear correspondingly larger and stronger in light than those in the background (or far distance).

The following sketches show three stages of analysis of a very complex vista, the busy harbor of Naples. Obviously, drastic reduction of the number of irrelevant objects seen in such a teeming landscape was required. This reduction of the "innumerable to the essential" is the guiding factor in making pictures. It has special application when the artist is confronted by the vast complexity of landscape.

Naples

This is another complex vista that required drastic reduction of detail not essential to the telling of this landscape's story. The chart-like first sketch is art shorthand. Such sketches, followed by simplified color notes, serve two purposes. The primary one is that the artist has analyzed the teeming activity and reduced it to plausible terms for painting. The second purpose is that the scene inevitably changes from moment to moment, and the notes help retain the original setting that first captivated the artist.

Artistic Shorthand

Villepache, SEE COLORPLATE ON PAGE **137**

The search for eye-pleasing movements must be diligent, but never at the expense of the emotional telling of the scene's impact upon the painter. Imbalance, where it is dramatic, is preferable to mechanical precision in planning.

Hokusai's classic stylized waves are a masterpiece of design.

TREES

All trees are not intrinsically beautiful. It is the eye and imagination of man that isolates the anarchic jumble of leaves and branches and "selects" that which is beautiful. He discards the incidental and the irrelevant.

The artist, unlike the passing nature-lover, is confronted with the task of expressing his selection in paint. It is not only the patent impossibility of painting every detail of leaves and branches, trunk and roots, which requires that selection. It is the task of the artist to "remake" that tree into an art object. Your painting of a tree must be a mathematical example: Actual tree, minus unnecessary detail, plus your creative eye, and your emotional response. Add, also, your technical skill and your special individual handwriting. These combined elements will produce a tree, perhaps totally unlike its natural source, but also, perhaps, a fine work of art.

The Starry Night *by Vincent van Gogh*

Always remember that *you,* not nature, are the master of the fate of your landscape painting. You may change, rearrange, eliminate, stress, or minimize what you see in the actual scene. The ends most important to be served are your creative impulses. Your vision, beholding the same scene as others, will become completely different from theirs in any case, so that the liberties you take are with your own inner picture of that scene.

Gauguin painted with feverish intensity, and at the same time with great intelligence. He relied more on vivid color than on light and shade for the suggestion of form or distance. Actual colors of objects in a landscape were secondary to "needed" colors—those which satisfied his painting purposes.

Japanese artists are unsurpassed in their ability to express the delicacy of foliage with a minimum of detail.

SEE COLORPLATE ON PAGE **138**

PAINTING PEOPLE

Portrait painting is not within the province of this book. Such portraits that have come down to us as "pictures," and these are very many, are not relevant because they are likenesses but because of their intrinsic qualities as painting. Most of Goya's sitters have faded into the obscurity of remote history but they live intensely as great pictures.

Painting people calls for more than faithful representation of the features of a particular person. At the outset the first consideration in painting people is: What do you wish to "say" about them? Are they incidental in the landscape? Are they to carry the burden of the picture story? Is the mood to be expressed shown in their faces or their carriage? Are they to be merely additional masses of form and color in the total design of your picture? These and many other considerations must be pondered before and during the evolving of your painting.

The posed model is less and less the source of figures in most painting. The invention of characters, if less literal in detail, allows for greater play of imagination. The decrease of devotion to realistic representation has freed the artist from the need for exact anatomy, and often similarity to the human form has become barely recognizable. However, along with departure from the literal came many intensely expressive figures, painted with emotion rather than "truth."

If we could look at the human figure unbiased by love and charity, we would be in a constant state of shock. Most figures we see are caricatures far beyond the feeble distortions of the satiric artist. If we had the objectivity to examine human design dispassionately we would discover that the surrealists lack imagination when contrasted to nature's grim wit. The artist has invented the classic figure along with distorted figures. The so-called truth lies somewhere in between.

Other books deal with color mixing and the nature of the chemical compound of pigments. It is hoped that the color plates in this book will convey the message that color is an essential construction material in the making of a picture. It must contribute to the whole or it will disturb the whole. Sheer reason can never govern the choice of color used by an artist. Unconscious forces are always contributing factors. The local color of a scene or character to be depicted is only an incidental influence. "Real" color and created color are rarely identical. Nature's impulses are not remotely similar to those of humans, and it would be strange indeed if the results were more than similar.

The Male Animal, SEE COLORPLATE ON PAGE **140**   **PAINTING PEOPLE**

Trio, SEE COLORPLATE ON PAGE 141

In using color you need not slavishly try to follow the intrinsic color of objects about you. Artists have found that where green skin enhances the impact of the painting, so-called "flesh color" is expendable. If purple horses give desired power to a painting, nature's limited range of horse colors may be replaced. This is not to suggest that whim or arbitrary decisions should be the guide and that all color suggested by nature should be automatically changed. Careful consideration should always temper impluse. That which serves the picture story, the emotional message, and the compositional needs must enter into color decisions along with unconscious drives and intuitive taste.

The process of combining two or more figures in a composition so that they "live together" believably is essentially one of imagination. To pose several figures in a group and draw from that group is impractical. Even where it is feasible, the results would probably be static and dull. Group-posed procedure is occasionally used for a family portrait, but rarely in a picture that requires movement and the spontaneity of life.

The series that follows begins with the first "play" with figure arrangement. It progresses until the ultimate composition is decided upon. Then follows the steps in the progress of the painting until the picture could, in the opinion of the painter, be called finished.

Here is a series of relatively conventional figure forms shown in various stages of painting progress. The purpose of the figures is to demonstrate the process of simplification as an aid in the construction of solid form. Virtually all extraneous detail has been eliminated in favor of essential construction. If you have live, posing models available, by all means study and paint from them, but it is also of great value to imagine and invent figures. The paintings of such figures will inevitably have directness and personal expression frequently lost in the paintings from life.

The Record Player

The heads shown here are not merely structural exercises. An effort has been made to demonstrate the structural application of paint to produce a sculptural quality along with emotional expression. The use of light and shade, the character of the impasto, and the suggestion of dramatic facial expression are all intended to contribute to the picture story. Study these plates and paint a series of heads (your own in the mirror if no other model is available) expressing some emotional "story."

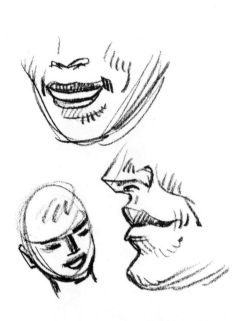

Quartet *by Jan De Ruth*

The age-old theme of mother and child has been painted from every emotional viewpoint, religious, social, sentimental, and primitive. The theme attracts because there is an elemental "rightness" of design in the classic mother-and-child pose as well as a challenging contrast of age factors. As subject matter, it would be difficult to find a more stimulating theme. Try a few arrangements of the mother-and-child combination making a strong effort to express how you feel about that subject.

SEE COLORPLATE ON PAGE **142**

Most of the plates in this book show the preference of this painter for the recognizable "object"—human, animal, or any "natural" manifestation. This preference, it is hoped, has not excluded a deep interest in achieving qualities more abstract than the mere depiction of these objects. Every well-conceived painting must have elements of the nonobjective, no matter how literal the subject. These nonobjective elements reveal themselves in the rhythms, color relationships, relation of mass to mass, and in the "totality" of the painting, which should, if it is good, be greater than the sum of all its parts.

For those students whose interests lie in a less literal picture story, the study of these elements is available. As to the so-called literal elements, that is, the depiction of people and things, no artist can hope (nor should he wish) to reproduce on his canvas, an exact copy of the object depicted. He must use what he sees and paraphrase it to the point that it becomes a creation of his own. This process is inevitable. The good quality of that creation is *not* inevitable. To have that virtue it must pass through the filter of the artist's skills, tastes, and emotions.

Virtually all we know of past civilizations has come from their art. The richest sources were those which depicted man and his surroundings. The most enlightening knowledge came from those art works which evoked the emotions of the period rather than the outer aspects.

We can be sure that the Greeks did not all look like the magnificent examples in their sculpture, but we know a great deal of the prevailing spirit through those countless fine works of art. It is, furthermore, a tragic loss to mankind that religious taboos barring figure depiction created almost a virtual art vacuum between the high creative period of Biblical days until a relatively recent period when those taboos ceased to be so severe. A similar loss of creative talent resulted from taboos against the depiction of humans and animals among the Arab peoples. Fortunately, the human figure has come back into art fashions and the study of figure painting has regained respectability.

A number of the following pages are devoted to basic figure construction in paint. Study them and paint figures utilizing some of the simplifications demonstrated. Then try using them in a painting so that they live together and tell a picture story.

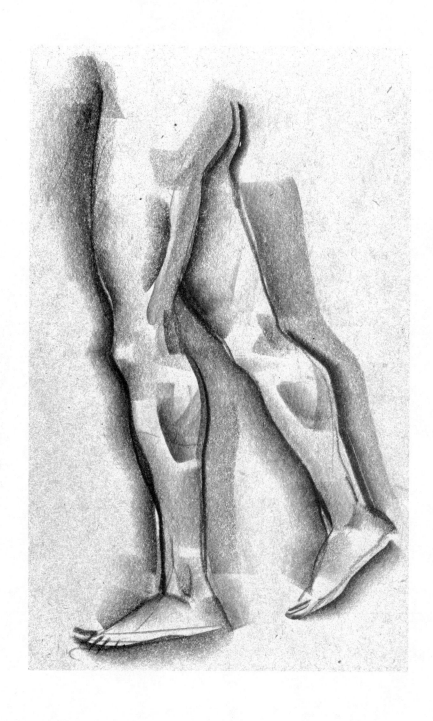

Three Women at the Spring *by Pablo Picasso*

A story picture by Picasso done in his neoclassic period.

No serious artist can be so catholic in his tastes that all schools of art are of equal interest to him to the point where he has painted in the manner of all those schools. The list of schools of painting is enormous and growing at an accelerated rate. This acceleration is due, in no small part, to the market. Madison Avenue is ever on the hunt for the sensational and new. Unhappily, artists are not immune to the call of that source of fame and money.

A frequent result of the "eye on the market and ear to the ground" attitude of many students and even "finished" artists, is loss of personality. Its replacement is the assumed mannerisms of the currently popular. What is even worse, in the search for quick recognition and success, many students spend most of their painting energy trying to be daring and different.

It must be admitted that out of this wild hunt many striking paintings of high quality have evolved, but far more potentially fine painters are drowned in the vortex of this sea of sensationalism. Honest preference for any of these schools, even the most sensational, is certainly permissible. The searching artist is sympathetic to all good art and cannot be arbitrary in his attitudes toward any school of painting, but empathy for any one of them must be based on more than the fact that it is the current rage.

First studies for "The Girls." Notice that after some consideration the positions were changed and the characters developed. The preliminary sketches are the rehearsal stage for painting and the final painting should not be started until you have satisfied yourself with the staging of your story.

The Girls

First study for the opera interior for the painting that follows.

The vista is expanded and the stage is set for the completion of the painting on the next page.

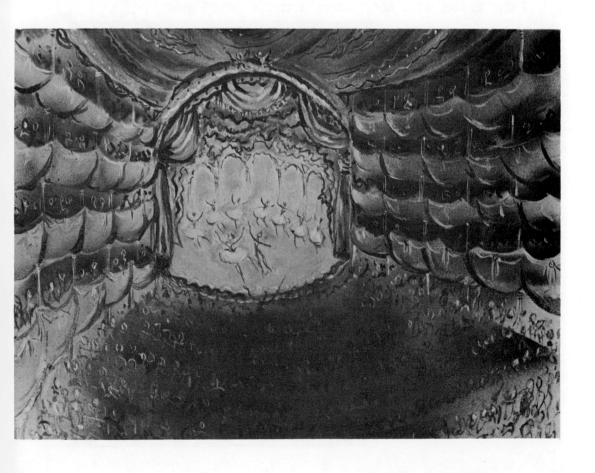

Detail of "Fledermaus." Although there is a great deal of detail in this painting, only the dramatic areas of the story were painted in light in an effort to enhance that drama by strong contrasts of gloom and brilliance.

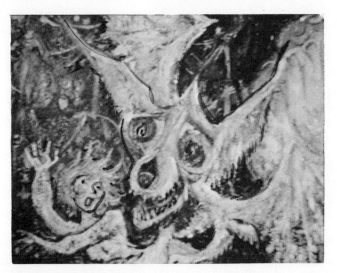

An early stage of the painting opposite.

These figures were not painted from the posed model.

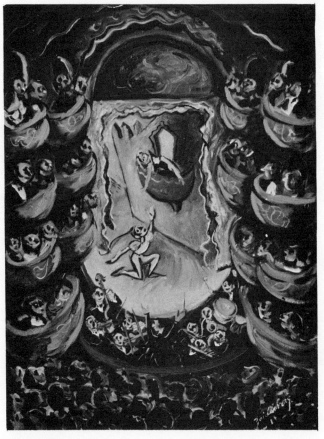

Curious Incident at the "Fledermaus",
SEE COLORPLATE ON PAGE 155

The Box, SEE COLORPLATE ON PAGE **144**

Big Game, SEE COLORPLATE ON PAGE **145**

Although practice in drawing from living models is a valuable experience, necessary for your studies, the "invented" figure is far more likely to come alive in a painting. Posed models are only spontaneous for the first few minutes of a pose and then they become rigid with effort. That unnatural quality may very well be transferred to your canvas.

The following compositions are examples of "invented" figures conceived in an effort to make them "live together." It is obviously impossible to gather a living group and ask them to pose for hours as you work out your complex composition problems and do the actual detail painting. Many artists make quick sketches for each pose from living models but these, too, must be modified or exaggerated to serve the picture's needs.

Sea Shells *by Jan De Ruth*

Awakening *by Jan De Ruth*

Chapters End *by Jan De Ruth*

THE ART LIFE

That all artists are unconventional is as it should be. This does not imply that Bohemian living is necessary to the artist or that he be deliberately eccentric. It means that if he feels and thinks as an artist he is a full-time creative person and his way of life will inevitably be creative.

There are many fine Sunday painters but, in a way, that approach is a contradiction of terms. The painter in the unfortunate position of not being able to devote full time to his art, must, for the sake of that art, consider himself a week-day worker and a *full-time* creator. In other words, the way of life for an art student as well as for an artist must be always involved with the creative process even if the hours available for actual easel work are few.

The fact that Gauguin abandoned his life as a broker and a husband and father does not suggest that unconventionality need follow such drastic lines as soon as a man becomes a painter. Most good painters live relatively sedate lives and make good fathers and husbands (or wives and mothers). The point to be stressed, however, is that one must be a conscious artist every moment and that all one thinks and does must consciously or unconsciously contribute to one's painting life.

Begin to think as an artist, see as an artist, and even at your desk or in the kitchen, live the artist's life—creatively.

The Round Table

COLORPLATES

Respite

Curious Incident at the "Fledermaus"

The Box

Big Game

DRY LAND

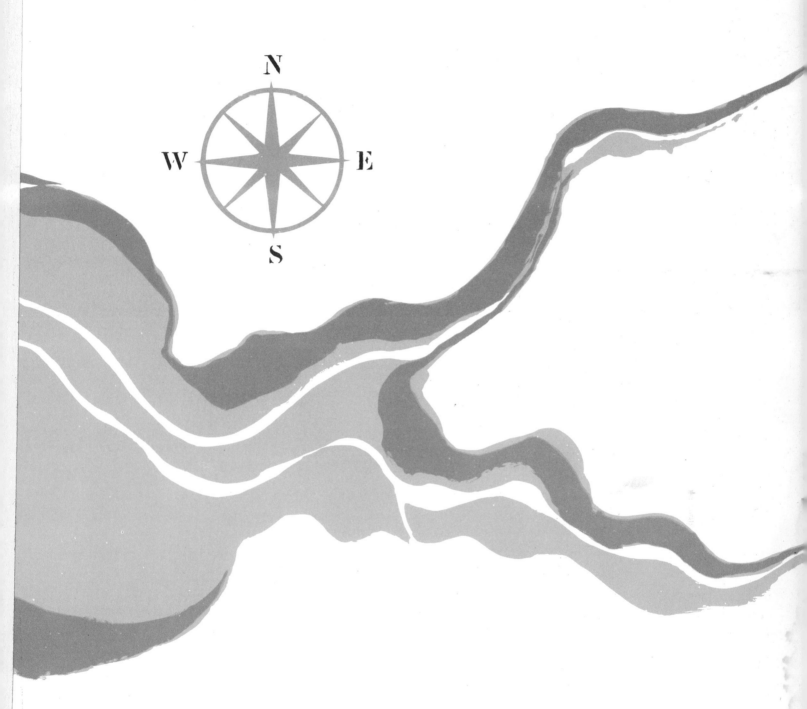

First published in Great Britain in 1966 by
Macdonald & Co (Publishers) Ltd.
Gulf House, 2 Portman Street, London, W.1
First distribution in the United States of America
by McGraw-Hill Book Company, 1966
Library of Congress Catalog Card Number : 66-11942
Printed in Italy by Officine Grafiche Arnoldo Mondadori Editore, Verona

Napoli

adventure
at Mont-Saint-Michel

McGraw-Hill Book Company
New York   San Francisco

Centaurée lives in a small thatched cottage.   Yan lives
nearby.   Their houses nestle beside a bay on the sandy
coast of Normandy in France.   At high tide the sea comes

6

almost to their doors.   When it goes out, it disappears
right over the horizon, leaving only sand.   Centaurée longs
to know where the sea goes.

Both Centaurée's father and Yan's father are fishermen. Early each morning they set their nets in the streams that twist and turn through the sands. Every evening they haul in their nets and take their catch across the bay to sell it on the island of Mont-Saint-Michel.

Yan's grandfather is now too old to go fishing, but when the sun shines he sits outside and mends nets.

He has made many voyages and tells the children about

islands covered in flowers, about terrible storms and about coasts from which the sea never disappears.

"Once," he says, "when I was young, I saw whole houses swept away by the sea."

Centaurée and Yan listen enthralled. Yan's grandfather knows all there is to know about sand, wind and tide. But he never tells them what lies beyond the horizon. He never explains where the sea goes and why it comes back.

Every day Centaurée sorts from the baskets all fish too

small to be sold, while her mother cooks freshly
caught shellfish for the family.

Centaurée is always there to watch when the fishermen
set out, wishing that she could follow them over the horizon

to discover where the sea goes and what makes it come back.   One day she takes butter and bread, pulls on a sweater, and...

...off she goes.

From time to time she stops to pick up black, glistening seashells or watches clouds of gulls circle and then alight on the sand. She walks farther on and hears a faint plopping ahead of her in the sand. She crouches to listen and sees a tiny hole in the sand. When she digs with her finger she finds a small scallop — and another! — and another!...

When she can carry no more, Centaurée moves on, delighted with her first catch. But suddenly one of her feet

sinks into the sand, then the other, and in a moment she is up to her knees in it — a prisoner.

Centaurée is very frightened. She remembers how Yan's grandfather warned, "Out there is sucking mud. If you get caught in it, you must not hesitate. Throw yourself flat and crawl out on your stomach."

Centaurée throws herself flat, then scrambles clear, but drops her scallops as she runs for safety.

Centaurée wades through several streams and suddenly recognizes some nets mended by Yan's grandfather. But they are empty. The fishermen have come and gone. Centaurée looks around. She cannot see the shore, the houses, even the streams. Centaurée feels tired and frightened as the beach grows dark. She remembers how the tide sweeps across the sands in a great wave, fast as a galloping horse.

Terrified, she stumbles breathlessly toward the tiny group of rocks called Tombelaine.

She reaches Tombelaine, scrambles over rocks, climbs up and up, brambles tearing at her clothes. Black cormorants sail overhead. Perhaps now she will see her home or the fishermen.

But the sea is already sweeping around her island. Wave follows wave with a ceaseless roar like a distant storm.

The sea rolls back the waters of the streams as though they were not there.

Meanwhile, Yan has missed Centaurée. He goes to her house, but it is empty. Worried, he begins a thorough search. Looking out at the sucking sand, he sees a line of small footprints. He calls as loud as he can. Now the gulls are flying inshore and he knows the sea will soon follow. His heart in his mouth, Yan races for Mont-Saint-Michel to get help.

In the town the water has already flowed in through the gate at the end of the street. The fish are all sold. Now tourists are arriving by boat from the mainland and being carried ashore by the fishermen.

At Yan's news the fishermen stop everything to get one of their boats to sea. They race off for Tombelaine.

Huddled against a rock, Centaurée hears grass rust-
ling, waves slapping and shushing. Suddenly she hears faint
voices calling her name. She slithers wildly down the rocks
and leaps into the waiting arms of a fisherman.

It is dark when the boat reaches port, but the jetty is crowded with people. They all rush forward to hug and kiss Centaurée and question her, but Yan says, "You must be cold and hungry. Come up to the Café Sirène."

27

In the café the fishermen try to explain to her. "The horizon isn't a line. It moves when you move. The earth is round, Centaurée. It turns and so the water moves. The moon also turns..."

Centaurée is very sleepy. She feels that everything round her is turning too. Faintly she hears Yan's grandfather saying, "I warned you it was dangerous!"

But grandfathers always say that...